for

COMMON GOOD
COMMON GROUND

BUILDING COMMITMENT
& COMMUNITY

Edited by
Dr. Stuart C. Lord, Ryan Hays,
Kelly Haley, & Wayne Meisel

Designed by Lesley Ehlers

PETER PAUPER PRESS, INC.
WHITE PLAINS, NEW YORK

Text copyright © 1999
Peter Pauper Press, Inc.
202 Mamaroneck Avenue
White Plains, NY 10601
All rights reserved
ISBN 0-88088-107-0
Printed in China
7 6 5 4 3 2 1

Common Good—Common Ground is a book
about community. It urges its readers, individually and
collectively, to restore community as an essential
element of American life.

Before we can restore our fragmented communities,
however, we must first have a shared understanding of
what community means. Community is not a coalescing
of individuals who look alike and think alike.
Community is not a place where people are robbed of
their uniqueness, culture and heritage. Community does
not require us to blend our similarities and ignore our
differences.

Community is an amazing gathering place, a wishing
well for our thoughts, our hopes, our fears and our
dreams. Community is a place where people are free to
learn, explore, create and build; free to celebrate and to
work; and where individuals, families and cultures are
treated with justice, equality and respect. Community
invites members from all walks of life not only to have a
voice, but to share that voice. Community recognizes our
similarities and celebrates our differences. Community
fosters a shared understanding, an appreciation for
cultural and intellectual diversity.

Once we have started to think together, we must act
together. The most distinctive virtue of any community
is its ability to mobilize and collectively work for the

common good, ensuring that all members of the community have an equal opportunity to live, learn, serve, and grow. Each and every member of a community is accountable and has a shared responsibility to contribute. Through our shared responsibility to love, educate, collaborate, lead, and serve, we can build common ground on which to stand.

From our shared understanding of diversity and our shared responsibility of action comes a shared destiny. We are one people, endowed by the richness of all cultures, bound by the laws of interdependence, and impelled by the hope of creating unity-in-difference. We are distinctively different, yet unequivocally united. We have a common origin and a common destiny.

Common Good—Common Ground is a collection that captures the essence of community. It is intended to challenge the reader to foster a shared understanding, commit to a shared responsibility and embrace a shared destiny. The editors and authors of this work have gathered the voices of their own histories and heritages and created this book—a feast and celebration of words, ideas and inspiration.

S. C. L.
R. H.
K. H.
W. M.

Shared Understanding

UNITY

What lies behind us and what lies before us are tiny matters compared to what lies within us.

OLIVER WENDELL HOLMES

Someday after mastering the winds, the waves, the tides and gravity, we shall harness for God the energies of love. And then for the second time in the history of the world, man will have discovered fire.

PIERRE TEILHARD DE CHARDIN

[Y]ou can love completely without complete understanding.

NORMAN MACLEAN,
A River Runs Through It

What you get is a living—what you give is a life.

LILLIAN GISH

You don't have to blow out the other fellow's light to let your own shine.

BERNARD BARUCH

When you come right down to it, the secret of having it all is loving it all.

DR. JOYCE BROTHERS

When you cease to make a contribution, you begin to die.

ELEANOR ROOSEVELT

I am a little pencil in the hand of a writing God who is sending a love letter to the world.

MOTHER TERESA

Give me where to stand, and I will move the earth.

ARCHIMEDES

Only a life lived for others is a life worth while.

ALBERT EINSTEIN

We can easily forgive a child who is afraid of the dark; the real tragedy of life is when adults are afraid of the light.

PLATO

How far that little candle throws his beams!
So shines a good deed in a naughty world.

WILLIAM SHAKESPEARE,
The Merchant of Venice

A thing is bigger for being shared.

GAELIC PROVERB

Real generosity is doing something nice for someone who'll never find it out.

FRANK A. CLARK

Kindness is the language which the deaf can hear and the blind can see.

MARK TWAIN

Charity is a virtue of the heart and not of the hand.

AMERICAN PROVERB

The only gift is a portion of thyself.

RALPH WALDO EMERSON

It's easy to make a buck. It's a lot tougher to make a difference.

TOM BROKAW

No one owns life, but anyone who can pick up a frying pan owns death.

WILLIAM BURROUGHS

In the hope of reaching the moon men fail to see the flowers that blossom at their feet.

ALBERT SCHWEITZER

When elephants fight it is the grass that suffers.

KIKUYU PROVERB

What counts is not necessarily the size of the dog in the fight—it's the size of the fight in the dog.

DWIGHT D. EISENHOWER

None preaches better than the ant, and she says nothing.

BENJAMIN FRANKLIN

The strength of the pack is the wolf,
And the strength of the wolf is the pack.

RUDYARD KIPLING

A river passes through many countries and each claims it for its own. But there is only one river.

A SUFI MASTER

What is success?

To laugh often and much;

To win the respect of intelligent people and the affection of children;

To earn the appreciation of honest critics and endure the betrayal of false friends;

To appreciate beauty;

To find the best in others;

To leave the world a bit better, whether by a healthy child, a garden patch or a redeemed social condition;

To know even one life has breathed easier because you have lived;

That is to have succeeded.

RALPH WALDO EMERSON

The friend who understands you, creates you.

ROMAIN ROLLAND

There was never a person who did anything worth doing that did not receive more than he gave.

HENRY WARD BEECHER

It is by spending one's self that one becomes rich.

SARAH BERNHARDT

Perfect happiness is the absence of striving for happiness.

CHUANG-TSE

One cannot step twice into the same river.

HERAKLEITOS

If the only prayer you say in your whole life is "thank you," that would suffice.

MEISTER ECKHART

Things which matter most must never be at the mercy of things which matter least.

GOETHE

When I let go of what I am, I become what I might be. When I let go of what I have, I receive what I need.

JOHN HEIDER

The world is too dangerous for anything but truth and too small for anything but love.

WILLIAM SLOAN COFFIN

We ourselves feel that what we are doing is just a drop in the ocean. But the ocean would be less because of that missing drop.

MOTHER TERESA

A journey of a thousand miles must begin with a single step.

LAO-TZU

The real voyage of discovery consists not in seeking new landscapes, but in having new eyes.

MARCEL PROUST

[D]iversity remains America's most prominent virtue and its most unsettling problem.

BENJAMIN R. BARBER

Do not free a camel of the burden of his hump; you may be freeing him from being a camel.

G. K. CHESTERTON

Everybody hears a different drummer.

ALVIN AILEY

You don't get harmony when everybody sings the same note.

DOUG FLOYD

I am invisible, understand, simply because people refuse to see me.

RALPH ELLISON

We don't see things as they are, we see them as we are.

ANAÏS NIN

It's the things in common that make relationships enjoyable, but it's the little differences that make them interesting.

TODD RUTHMAN

We all live under the same sky, but we don't have the same horizon.

KONRAD ADENAUER

He who does not understand your silence will probably not understand your words.

ELBERT HUBBARD

I freed thousands of slaves, I could have freed thousands more, if they had known they were slaves.

HARRIET TUBMAN

An optimist is a person who sees a green light everywhere, while the pessimist sees only the red stoplight. . . . The truly wise person is colorblind.

ALBERT SCHWEITZER

I love everybody now that I have grey hair.

CHIEF POLATKIN (SPOKANE GARRY)

Service to others is the rent you pay for your room here on earth.

MUHAMMAD ALI

The ends you serve that are selfish will take you no further than yourself; but the ends you serve that are for all, in common, will take you even into eternity.

MARCUS GARVEY

No person was ever honored for what he received. Honor has been received for what he gave.

CALVIN COOLIDGE

When I am employed in serving others, I do not look upon myself as conferring favors but paying debts.

BENJAMIN FRANKLIN

Caring for persons, the more able and the less able serving each other, is the rock upon which a good society is built.

ROBERT K. GREENLEAF

Genuine community is real when it reaches out to heal. We have only begun to understand the world's pain and the urgency of responding to it.

SAMUEL PROCTOR

It is better to light one small candle than to curse the darkness.

CONFUCIUS

He who lives only for himself is truly dead to others.

PUBLILIUS SYRUS

I look to a time when brotherhood needs no publicity, to a time when a brotherhood award would be as ridiculous as an award for getting up each morning.

DANIEL D. MICH

The best and most beautiful things in the world
cannot be seen or even touched. They must be
felt with the heart.

HELEN KELLER

Justice is my being allowed to do whatever I like.
Injustice is whatever prevents my doing so.

SAMUEL BUTLER

The earth is the mother of all people, and all
people should have equal rights upon it. You might
as well expect the rivers to run backward as that
any man who was born a free man should be
contented when penned up and denied liberty to go
where he pleases.

CHIEF JOSEPH (NEZ PERCÉ)

Justice, I firmly believe, is so subtle a thing that to
interpret it one has only need of a heart.

JOSÉ GARCÍA OLIVER

In matters concerning yourself, trust first your head; in matters concerning others, trust first your heart.

AMERICAN PROVERB

Compassion is the ultimate and most meaningful embodiment of emotional maturity. It is through compassion that a person achieves the highest peak and deepest reach in his or her search for self-fulfillment.

ARTHUR JERSILD

The giving of love is an education in itself.

ELEANOR ROOSEVELT

The entire sum of existence is the magic of being needed by just one person.

VI PUTNAM

Love alone is capable of uniting living beings in such a way as to complete and fulfill them, for it alone takes them and joins them by what is deepest in themselves.

PIERRE TEILHARD DE CHARDIN

Not what we give, but what we share makes us great.

AMERICAN PROVERB

I take as my guide the hope of a saint: in crucial things, unity—in important things, diversity—in all things, generosity.

GEORGE BUSH

Nothing can dim the light which shines from within.

MAYA ANGELOU

In every child who is born, under no matter what
circumstances, and of no matter what parents, the
potentiality of the human race is born again.

JAMES AGEE

If I am not for myself, who will be for me?
If I am for myself only, what am I?
If not now—when?

BABYLONIAN TALMUD

I expect to pass through life but once. If, therefore,
there be any kindness I can show, or any good
thing I can do for any fellow being, let me do it
now . . . as I shall not pass this way again.

WILLIAM PENN

Shared Responsibility

What do we live for, if it is not to make life less difficult for each other?

GEORGE ELIOT

Every man must decide whether he will walk in the light of creative altruism or the darkness of destructive selfishness. This is the judgment. Life's most persistent and urgent question is, What are you doing for others?

MARTIN LUTHER KING, JR.

I must first be the change I want to see in my world.

GANDHI

To live is good. To live vividly is better. To live vividly together is best.

MAX EASTMAN

No man can live happily who regards himself alone, who turns everything to his own advantage. Thou must live for another if thou wishest to live for thyself.

SENECA

In my religion, Hinduism, the Bhagavad Gita says if you do not give something to the community, then you are a thief.

NITA SHAH

We must not only give what we have; we must also give what we are.

DÉSIRÉ-JOSEPH MERCIER

There is no exercise better for the heart than reaching down and lifting people up.

JOHN ANDREW HOLMER

The life of a man consists not in seeing visions and in dreaming dreams, but in active charity and in willing service.

HENRY WADSWORTH LONGFELLOW

In our era, the road to holiness necessarily passes through the world of action.

DAG HAMMARSKJÖLD

Everybody can be great. Because anybody can serve. You don't have to have a college degree to serve. You don't have to make your subject and your verb agree to serve. You don't have to know about Plato and Aristotle to serve. You don't have to know Einstein's theory of relativity to serve. You don't have to know the second theory of thermodynamics in physics to serve. You only need a heart full of grace. A soul generated by love.

MARTIN LUTHER KING, JR.

Love in action is the answer to every problem in our lives and in this world. Love in action is the force that helped us make it to this place, and it's the truth that will set us free.

SUSAN TAYLOR

Love conquers all things. . . .

VIRGIL

Life is just a short walk from the cradle to the grave—and it sure behooves us to be kind to one another along the way.

ALICE CHILDRESS

In the time we have it is surely our duty to do all the good we can to all the people we can in all the ways we can.

WILLIAM BARCLAY

Love is a verb.

CLARE BOOTHE LUCE

Life is a great big canvas, and you should throw all the paint on it you can.

DANNY KAYE

Treat people as if they were what they should be, and you help them become what they are capable of becoming.

GOETHE

A friend loves at all times . . .

PROVERBS 17:17 NKJV

Treat your friends as you do your pictures, and place them in their best light.

JENNIE JEROME CHURCHILL

Love is, above all, the gift of oneself.

JEAN ANOUILH

Now join your hands, and with your hands your hearts.

WILLIAM SHAKESPEARE,
Henry VI, Part III

We can only learn to love by loving.

IRIS MURDOCH

Actions and words are the windows through which the heart is seen.

AMERICAN PROVERB

If your neighbor can't smile, lend him yours.

AMERICAN PROVERB

Coming together is a beginning; keeping together is progress; working together is success.

HENRY FORD

The secret is to work less as individuals and more as a team. As a coach I play not my eleven best, but my best eleven.

KNUTE ROCKNE

To lead the people, walk behind them.

LAO-TZU

Flatter me, and I may not believe you. Criticize me, and I may not like you. Ignore me, and I may not forgive you. Encourage me, and I will not forget you.

WILLIAM ARTHUR WARD

A community is like a ship; everyone ought to be prepared to take the helm.

HENRIK IBSEN

Community requires us to ease the suffering of those who are most victimized, whoever and wherever they are.

SAMUEL PROCTOR

Charity looks at the need, not at the cause.

GERMAN PROVERB

A man is called selfish not for pursuing his own good, but for neglecting his neighbor's.

RICHARD WHATELY

It is not enough to help the feeble up, but to support him after.

AMERICAN PROVERB

Who is a holy person? The one who is aware of others' suffering.

KABIR

Pray for the dead and fight like hell for the living.

"MOTHER" MARY JONES

Assuredly, I say to you, inasmuch as you did it to one of the least of these My brethren, you did it to Me.

MATTHEW 25:40 NKJV

The vocation of every man and woman . . . to serve other people.

LEO TOLSTOY

My goal is this: always to put myself in the place in which I am best able to serve, wherever my gifts and qualities find the best soil, the widest field of action. There is no other goal.

HERMANN HESSE

Action is the antidote to despair.

JOAN BAEZ

An ounce of action is worth a ton of theory.

FRIEDRICH ENGELS

It should be our purpose in life to see that each of us makes such a contribution as will enable us to say that we, individually and collectively, are a part of the answer to the world problem and not part of the problem itself.

ANDREW CORDIER

We come to reason, not to dominate. We do not seek to have our way, but to find a common way.

LYNDON BAINES JOHNSON

If we cannot end now our differences, at least we can help make the world safe for diversity.

JOHN F. KENNEDY

You don't fight racism with racism, the best way to fight racism is with solidarity.

BOBBY SEALE

When I liberate others, I liberate myself.

FANNIE LOU HAMER

Charity begins at home, and justice begins next door.

CHARLES DICKENS

Who ever walked behind anyone to freedom? If we can't go hand in hand, I don't want to go.

HAZEL SCOTT

Divide and conquer, in our world, must become
define and empower.

AUDRE LORDE

Peace starts within each one of us.

THE DALAI LAMA

Attend to self reform and social reform will take
care of itself.

RAMANA MAHARSHI

O mankind, we have created you male and female,
and made you races and tribes, that you may show
mutual recognition.

THE KORAN

We must turn to each other and not on each other.

JESSE JACKSON

The only way out of today's misery is for people to become worthy of each other's trust.

ALBERT SCHWEITZER

Be careful how you live; you may be the only Bible some people will ever read.

JO PETTY

Every man feels instinctively that all the beautiful sentiments in the world weigh less than a single lovely action.

JAMES RUSSELL LOWELL

The shortest answer is doing.

ENGLISH PROVERB

America built the Panama Canal, split the atom, developed the polio vaccine, explored outer space. And yet, our kids aren't learning to read and write.

LEE IACCOCA

We don't inherit the land from our ancestors. We borrow it from our children.

PENNSYLVANIA DUTCH SAYING

It takes a whole village to raise a single child.

YORUBA PROVERB

If there is anything that we wish to change in the child, we should first examine it and see whether it is not something that could better be changed in ourselves.

CARL GUSTAV JUNG

Education is our passport to the future, for tomorrow belongs to the people who prepare for it today.

MALCOLM X

If opportunity doesn't knock, build a door.

MILTON BERLE

It's better to look ahead and prepare than to look back and regret.

JACKIE JOYNER-KERSEE

Think wrongly, if you please, but in all cases think for yourself.

DORIS LESSING

Let the beauty we love be what we do.

RUMI

I may suggest that God did not bear the Cross only 1900 years ago, but He bears it today. . . . Do not then preach the God of history, but show Him as He lives today through you. . . . It is better to allow our lives to speak for us than our words.

GANDHI

Give gifts to those who should know love.

NTOZAKE SHANGE

We must stand together; if we don't, there will be no victory for any one of us.

"MOTHER" MARY JONES

The price of greatness is responsibility.

WINSTON CHURCHILL

Do not follow where the path may lead. Go instead where there is no path and leave a trail.

MURIEL STRODE

Never let your head hang down. Never give up and sit down and grieve. Find another way. And don't pray when it rains if you don't pray when the sun shines.

SATCHEL PAIGE

Shared
Destiny

We are a nation of communities, of tens
and tens of thousands of ethnic, religious,
social, business, labor union, neighborhood,
regional and other organizations, all of them
varied, voluntary, and unique . . . a brilliant
diversity spread like stars, like a thousand
points of light in a broad and peaceful sky.
GEORGE BUSH

Destiny is no matter of chance. It is a matter of choice: It is not a thing to be waited for, it is a thing to be achieved.

WILLIAM JENNINGS BRYAN

It is in the shelter of each other that the people live.

IRISH PROVERB

To exist is to co-exist.

GABRIEL MARCEL

We cannot hold a torch to light another's path without brightening our own.

BEN SWEETLAND

To live in society doesn't mean simply living side by side with others in a more or less close cohesion; it means living through one another and for one another.

PAUL-EUGENE ROY

When you learn to live for others, they will live for you.

PARAMAHANSA YOGANANDA

If God be for us who can be against us?

DESMOND TUTU

When we pay attention to nature's music, we find that everything on the earth contributes to its harmony.

HAZRAT INAYAT KHAN

Humanity participates by nature in all cosmic events, and is inwardly as well as outwardly interwoven with them.

RICHARD WILHELM

Things derive their being and nature by mutual dependence and are nothing in themselves.

NAGARJUNA

It just seems to me that as long as we are both here, it's pretty clear that the struggle is to share the planet, rather than to divide it.

ALICE WALKER

America is not like a blanket—one piece of unbroken cloth. America is more like a quilt— many patches, many pieces, many colors, many sizes, all woven together by a common thread.

JESSE JACKSON

Everything the same; everything distinct.

ZEN PROVERB

I am a part of all that I have met.

ALFRED, LORD TENNYSON

The language of citizenship suggests that self-interests are always embedded in communities of action and that in serving neighbors one also serves oneself.

BENJAMIN R. BARBER

I want to be the white man's brother, not his brother-in-law.

MARTIN LUTHER KING, JR.

Once the game is over, the king and the pawn go
back into the same box.

ITALIAN SAYING

If the human race can begin to realize a common
origin today, then we can also begin to see anew
our common destiny and to act accordingly.

MATTHEW FOX

Religions are different roads converging upon the
same point. What does it matter that we take
different roads so long as we reach the same goal?

GANDHI

I'm not into isms and asms. There isn't a Catholic
moon and a Baptist sun. I know the universal God is
universal. . . . I feel that the same God-force that is
the mother and father of the pope is also the mother
and father of the loneliest wino on the planet.

DICK GREGORY

Religion is a candle inside a multicolored lantern. Everyone looks through a particular color, but the candle is always there.

MOHAMMED NAGUIB

The problems we face today, violent conflicts, destruction of nature, poverty, hunger, and so on, are human-created problems which can be resolved through human effort, understanding and development of a sense of brotherhood and sisterhood.

THE DALAI LAMA

In every community, there is work to be done. In every nation, there are wounds to heal. In every heart, there is the power to do it.

MARIANNE WILLIAMSON

To be free—to walk the good American earth as equal citizens, to live without fear, to enjoy the fruits of our toil, to give our children every opportunity in life—that dream which we have held so long in our hearts is today the destiny that we hold in our hands.

PAUL ROBESON

We cannot be separated in interest or divided in purpose. We stand together until the end.

WOODROW WILSON

One country, one constitution, one destiny.

DANIEL WEBSTER

United we stand, divided we fall.

G. P. MORRIS

Life is no brief candle to me. It is a sort of splendid torch which I've got hold of for the moment, and I want to make it burn as brightly as possible before handing it on to future generations.

GEORGE BERNARD SHAW

Give me your tired, your poor,

  Your huddled masses yearning
  to breathe free,

The wretched refuse of your teeming shore,

  Send these, the homeless,
  tempest-tossed, to me:

I lift my lamp beside the golden door!

EMMA LAZARUS

One generation plants the trees;
another gets the shade.

Nothing exists from whose nature some effect does not follow.

BARUCH SPINOZA

What the people of the city do not realize is that the roots of all living things are tied together.

CHAN K'IN VIEJO

We need to see the homeless for who they are and see that we need them as much as they need us. Only by recognizing that we're all roommates in the house of life together can we clean up our house and make it livable again.

WILLIAM LAWYER

Humanity participates by nature in all cosmic events, and is inwardly as well as outwardly interwoven with them.

RICHARD WILHELM

I have seen that in any great undertaking it is not enough for a man to depend simply upon himself.

LONE MAN (TETON SIOUX)

That is why true paths are essentially one path— because there is only one Spirit, one breath, one life, one energy in the universe. It belongs to none of us and all of us.

MATTHEW FOX

Peace is a never-ending process, the work of many decisions by many people in many countries. It is an attitude, a way of life, a way of solving problems and resolving conflicts. It cannot be forced on the smallest nation or enforced by the largest. It cannot ignore our differences or overlook our common interests. It requires us to work and live together.

OSCAR ARIAS SÁNCHEZ

A relationship is placing one's heart and soul in the hands of another while taking charge of another in one's soul and heart.

KAHLIL GIBRAN

Each friend represents a world in us, a world possibly not born until they arrive, and it is only by this meeting that a new world is born.

ANAÏS NIN

Today, as never before, the fates of men are so intimately linked to one another that a disaster for one is a disaster for everybody.

NATALIA GINZBURG

Americans all, we must bury the hatchet of discord and recognize that the only way to pull ourselves to higher ground is to pull together. We must blend hands, brains, emotions, talents, materials, machines into a mighty symphony of action for the common good.

WILFERD A. PETERSON

Mankind has become so much one family that we cannot insure our own prosperity except by insuring that of everyone else.

BERTRAND RUSSELL

Snowflakes, leaves, humans, plants, raindrops, stars, molecules, microscopic entities all come in communities. The singular cannot in reality exist.

PAULA GUNN ALLEN

We are all bound up together in one great bundle of humanity, and society cannot trample on the weakest and feeblest of its members without receiving the curse in its own soul.

FRANCES ELLEN WATKINS HARPER

I knew without a glimmer of doubt that all things in the universe were connected by a living truth that would not relent its continuing search for wholeness until every form of life was united.

LYNN V. ANDREWS

There are roads out of the secret places within us along which we all must move as we go to touch others.

ROMARE BEARDEN

One thing we know. Our God is the same God. This earth is precious to Him. Even the white man cannot be exempt from the common destiny. We may be brothers after all. We shall see.

CHIEF SEATTLE

I just want to do God's will. And He's allowed me to go up to the mountain. And I've looked over. And I've seen the promised land. I may not get there with you. But I want you to know tonight that we as a people will get to the promised land. And I'm happy tonight, I'm not worried about anything. I'm not fearing any man. Mine eyes have seen the glory of the coming of the Lord.

MARTIN LUTHER KING, JR.
April 3, 1968

The strongest and sweetest songs
yet remain to be sung.

WALT WHITMAN